Palo Alto Networks Certified Network Security Engineer (PCNSE) Exam Practice Questions & Dumps

Exam Practice Questions For Palo Alto Networks (PCNSE) Exam Prep LATEST VERSION

PRESENTED BY: Quantic Books

About Quantic Books:

Quantic Books is a publishing house based in Princeton, New Jersey, USA. , a platform that is accessible online as well as locally, which gives power to educational content, erudite collection, poetry & many other book genres. We make it easy for writers & authors to get their books designed, published, promoted, and sell professionally on worldwide scale with eBook + Print distribution. Quantic Books is now distributing books worldwide.

Note: Find answers of the questions at the last of the book.

QUESTION 1

Signify to the display.

An association has Palo Alto Networks NGFWs that deliver logs to remote monitoring and security management platforms. The network team has reported extreme traffic on the corporate WAN.

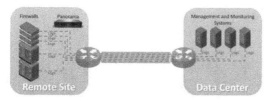

How might the Palo Alto Networks NGFW supervisor decline WAN traffic even upholding support for all the prevailing monitoring/security platforms?

A. Forward logs from firewalls only to Panorama and have Panorama forward logs to other external services.

B. Forward logs from external sources to Panorama for association, and from Panorama deliver them to the NGFW.

C. Organize log compression and optimization attributes on all remote firewalls.

D. Any arrangement on an M-500 would address the insufficient bandwidth concerns.

QUESTION 2

A supervisor has been requested to organize a Palo Alto Networks NGFW to give protection contrary to worms and trojans. Which Security Profile kind will protect contrary to worms and trojans?

A. Anti-Spyware
B. Instruction Prevention
C. File Blocking
D. Antivirus

QUESTION 3

A supervisor has been requested to organize active/passive HA for a pair of Palo Alto Networks NGFWs. The supervisor allocates priority 100 to the active firewall.

Which importance is accurate for the passive firewall?

A. 0
B. 99
C. 1
D. 255

QUESTION 4

If a template pile is allotted to a device and the pile comprises three templates with equivalent settings, which settings are published to the device when the template pile is pushed?

A. The settings allotted to the template that is on top of the pile.
B. The supervisor will be promoted to select the settings for that chosen firewall.
C. All the settings arranged in all templates.
D. Depending on the firewall location, Panorama chooses with settings to deliver.

QUESTION 5

Which procedure will with dynamism list tags on the Palo Alto Networks NGFW?

A. Alleviating API or the VMware API on the firewall or on the User-ID agent or the *ready-only domain controller*(RODC)
B. Alleviating API or the VMware API on the firewall or on the User-ID agent
C. XML API or the VMware API on the firewall or on the User-ID agent or the CLI
D. XML API or the VM Monitoring agent on the NGFW or on the User-ID agent

QUESTION 6

How does a supervisor program an Applications and Threats dynamic update even delaying installation of the update for a specific amount of time?

A. Organize the selection for "Threshold".
B. Deactivate automatic updates for the duration of weekdays.
C. Automatically "download only" and then install Applications and Threats later, after the supervisor approves the update.
D. Automatically "download and install" but with the "deactivate new applications" selection used.

QUESTION 7

Which two virtualization platforms legitimately support the deployment of Palo Alto Networks VM-Series firewalls? (Select two.)

A. Red Hat Enterprise Virtualization (RHEV)
B. Kernel Virtualization Module (KVM)
C. Boot Strap Virtualization Module (BSVM)
D. Microsoft Hyper-V

QUESTION 8

Which PAN-OS® policy needs you organize to force a user to give added IDs before he is permitted to access an internal application that comprises extremely-sensitive company data?

A. Security policy
B. Decryption policy
C. Verification policy
D. Application Override policy

QUESTION 9

A Security policy rule is arranged with a Vulnerability Protection Profile and an action of "Deny". Which action will this reason arrangement on the matched traffic?

A. The arrangement is illegal. The Profile Settings section will be grayed out when the Action is set to "Deny".

B. The arrangement will let the matched session unless a vulnerability signature is detected. The "Deny" action will supersede the per-severity defined actions defined in the associated Vulnerability Protection Profile.

C. The arrangement is illegal. It will reason the firewall to skip this Security policy rule. A warning will be displayed for the duration of a commit.

D. The arrangement is authentic. It will reason the firewall to deny the matched sessions. Any arranged Security Profiles have no effect if the Security policy rule action is set to "Deny".

QUESTION 10

A user's traffic traversing a Palo Alto Networks NGFW sometimes can reach http://www.company.com. At other times the session times out. The NGFW has been arranged with a PBF rule that the user's traffic matches when it goes to http://www.company.com.

How can the firewall be arranged automatically deactivate the PBF rule if the next hop goes down?

A. Make and add a Monitor Profile with an action of Wait Recover in the PBF rule in question.

B. Make and add a Monitor Profile with an action of Fail Over in the PBF rule in question.

C. Activate and organize a Link Monitoring Profile for the external interface of the firewall.

D. Organize path monitoring for the next hop gateway on the default route in the virtual router.

QUESTION 11

Which Captive Portal mode needs to be arranged to support MFA verification?

A. NTLM
B. Redirect
C. Single Sign-On
D. Transparent

QUESTION 12

A supervisor needs to execute an NGFW among their DMZ and Core network. EIGRP Routing among the two environments is needed. Which interface kind would support this company necessity?

A. Virtual Wire interfaces to permit EIGRP routing to remain among the Core and DMZ
B. Layer 3 or Aggregate Ethernet interfaces, but configuring EIGRP on subinterfaces only
C. Tunnel interfaces to terminate EIGRP routing on an IPsec tunnel (with the GlobalProtect License to support LSVPN and EIGRP protocols)
D. Layer 3 interfaces, but configuring EIGRP on the attached virtual router

QUESTION 13

A speed/duplex negotiation mismatch is among the Palo Alto Networks management port and the switch port which it connects. How would a supervisor organize the interface to 1Gbps?

A. set deviceconfig interface speed-duplex 1Gbps-full-duplex
B. set deviceconfig system speed-duplex 1Gbps-duplex
C. set deviceconfig system speed-duplex 1Gbps-full-duplex
D. set deviceconfig Interface speed-duplex 1Gbps-half-duplex

QUESTION 14

A web server is hosted in the DMZ, and the server is arranged to listen for incoming connections only on TCP port 8080. A Security policy rule letting access from the Trust zone to the DMZ zone need to be arranged to activate browsing access to the server.

Which application and service need to be arranged to let only cleartext web-browsing traffic to thins server on tcp/8080?

A. application: web-browsing; service: application-default
B. application: web-browsing; service: service-https
C. application: ssl; service: any
D. application: web-browsing; service: (custom with destination TCP port 8080)

QUESTION 15

In the image, what reasoned the commit warning?

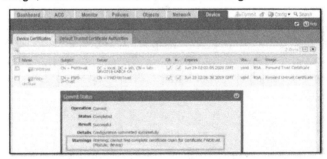

A. The CA license for FWDtrust has not been imported into the firewall.
B. The FWDtrust license has not been flagged as Trusted Root CA.
C. SSL Forward Proxy requires a public license to be imported into the firewall.
D. The FWDtrust license does not have a license chain.

QUESTION 16

Which procedure does a supervisor use to integrate all non-native MFA platforms in PAN-OS® software?

A. Okta
B. DUO
C. RADIUS
D. PingID

QUESTION 17

How would a supervisor monitor/capture traffic on the management interface of the Palo Alto Networks NGFW?

A. Use the debug data plane packet-diag set capture stage firewall file command.
B. Activate all four stages of traffic capture (TX, RX, DROP, Firewall).
C. Use the debug data plane packet-diag set capture stage management file command.
D. Use the tcpdump command.

QUESTION 18

A supervisor needs to enhance traffic to favor company-serious applications over non-serious applications. QoS natively integrates with which attribute to give service quality?

A. Port Inspection
B. License revocation
C. Content-ID
D. App-ID

QUESTION 19

A session in the Traffic log is reporting the application as "imperfect."
What does "imperfect" mean?

A. The three-way TCP handshake was observed, but the application
   might not be identified.
B. The three-way TCP handshake did not complete.
C. The traffic is approaching transversely UDP, and the application
   might not be identified.
D. Data was collected but was promptly discarded for the reason that
   of a Deny policy was applied before App-ID might be applied.

QUESTION 20

A supervisor needs to determine why users on the trust zone cannot reach specific websites. The only information available is shown on the given image. Which arrangement change must the supervisor make?

A.

B.

C.

D.

E.

QUESTION 21

A customer has an application that is being identified as unknown-tcp for one of their custom PostgreSQL database connections. Which two arrangement selections can be used to accurately categorize their custom database application? (Select two.)

A. Application Override policy.

B. Security policy to classify the custom application.

C. Custom application.

D. Custom Service object.

QUESTION 22

A supervisor has left a firewall to use the default port for all management services. Which three functions are done by the dataplane? (Select three.)

A. WildFire updates
B. NAT
C. NTP
D. antivirus
E. file blocking

QUESTION 23

A supervisor is using Panorama and numerous Palo Alto Networks NGFWs. After upgrading all devices to the latest PAN-OS® software, the supervisor allows log forwarding from the firewalls to Panorama. Pre-prevailing logs from the firewalls are not appearing in Panorama.

Which action would activate the firewalls to deliver their pre-prevailing logs to Panorama?

A. Use the import selection to pull logs into Panorama.
B. A CLI command will forward the pre-prevailing logs to Panorama.
C. Use the ACC to consolidate pre-prevailing logs.
D. The log database will need to exported form the firewalls and manually imported into Panorama.

QUESTION 24

A supervisor makes a custom application comprising Layer 7 signatures. The latest application and threat dynamic update is downloaded to the same NGFW. The update comprises an application that matches the same traffic signatures as the custom application.

Which application must be used to classify traffic traversing the NGFW?

A. Custom application
B. System logs show an application error and neither signature is used.
C. Downloaded application
D. Custom and downloaded application signature files are merged and both are used

QUESTION 25

Starting with PAN-OS version 9.1, GlobalProtect logging information is now recorded in which firewall log?

A. GlobalProtect
B. System
C. Verification
D. Arrangement

QUESTION 26

Which three verification services can a supervisor use to authenticate admins into the Palo Alto Networks NGFW without defining an equivalent admin account on the local firewall? (Select three.)

A. Kerberos
B. PAP
C. SAML
D. TACACS+
E. RADIUS
F. LDAP

QUESTION 27

Which Security policy rule will let an admin to block facebook chat but let Facebook in general?

A. Deny application facebook-chat before letting application facebook
B. Deny application facebook on top
C. Let application facebook on top
D. Let application facebook before denying application facebook-chat

QUESTION 28

A client is concerned about resource exhaustion for the reason that of denial-of-service attacks contrary to their DNS servers. Which selection will protect the specific servers?

A. Activate packet buffer protection on the Zone Protection Profile.
B. Apply an Anti-Spyware Profile with DNS sinkholing.
C. Use the DNS App-ID with application-default.
D. Apply a classified DoS Protection Profile.

QUESTION 29

A supervisor has users accessing network resources through Citrix XenApp 7.x.

Which User-ID mapping solution will map numerous users who are using Citrix to connect to the network and access resources?

A. Client Probing
B. Terminal Services agent
C. GlobalProtect
D. Syslog Monitoring

QUESTION 30

Which selection is part of the content inspection process?

A. Packet forwarding process
B. SSL Proxy re-encrypt
C. IPsec tunnel encryption
D. Packet egress process

QUESTION 31

Signify to the display.

Which licenses can be used as a Forward Trust license?

A. License from Default Trust License Authorities
B. Domain Sub-CA
C. Forward Trust
D. Domain-Root-Cert

QUESTION 32

Which selection would a supervisor select to define the license and protocol that Panorama and its handled devices use for SSL/TLS services?

A. Organize a Decryption Profile and select SSL/TLS services.
B. Set up SSL/TLS under **Policies > Service/URL Category > Service**.
C. Set up Security policy rule to let SSL communication.
D. Organize an SSL/TLS Profile.

QUESTION 33

Which CLI command can be used to export the tcpdump capture?

A. scp export tcpdump from mgmt.pcap to < username@host:path>
B. scp extract mgmt-pcap from mgmt.pcap to < username@host:path>
C. scp export mgmt-pcap from mgmt.pcap to < username@host:path>
D. download mgmt-pcap

QUESTION 34

Which tool gives a supervisor the skill to see tendencies in traffic over periods of time, such as threats detected in the last 30 days?

A. Session Browser
B. Application Command Center
C. TCP Dump
D. Packet Capture

QUESTION 35

Which three steps will decline the CPU utilization on the management plane? (Select three.)

A. Deactivate SNMP on the management interface.
B. Application override of SSL application.
C. Deactivate logging at session start in Security policies.
D. Deactivate predefined reports.
E. Decline the traffic being decrypted by the firewall.

QUESTION 36

Which attribute needs to you organize to prevent users from accidentally submitting their corporate IDs to a phishing website?

A. URL Filtering profile
B. Zone Protection profile
C. Anti-Spyware profile
D. Vulnerability Protection profile

QUESTION 37

How can a candidate or running arrangement be copied to a host external from Panorama?

A. Commit a running arrangement.
B. Save an arrangement snapshot.
C. Save a candidate arrangement.
D. Export a named arrangement snapshot.

QUESTION 38

The supervisor has allowed BGP on a virtual router on the Palo Alto Networks NGFW, but new routes do not seem to be populating the virtual router. Which two selections would help the supervisor troubleshoot this issue? (Select two.)

A. View the System logs and look for the error messages about BGP.
B. Perform a traffic pcap on the NGFW to see any BGP problems.
C. View the Runtime Stats and look for problems with BGP arrangement.
D. View the ACC tab to isolate routing issues.

QUESTION 39

A supervisor has allowed OSPF on a virtual router on the NGFW. OSPF is not adding new routes to the virtual router. Which two selections activate the supervisor to troubleshoot this issue? (Select two.)

A. View Runtime Stats in the virtual router.
B. View System logs.
C. Add a redistribution profile to forward as BGP updates.
D. Perform a traffic pcap at the routing stage.

QUESTION 40

Which three firewall states are authentic? (Select three.)

A. Active
B. Functional
C. Pending
D. Passive
E. Suspended

QUESTION 41

Which virtual router attribute regulates if a specific destination IP address is reachable?

A. Heartbeat Monitoring
B. Failover
C. Path Monitoring
D. Ping-Path

QUESTION 42

A supervisor has a necessity to export decrypted traffic from the Palo Alto Networks NGFW to a third-party, deep-level packet inspection appliance. Which interface kind and license attribute are necessary to meet the necessity?

A. Decryption Mirror interface with the Threat Analysis license
B. Virtual Wire interface with the Decryption Port Export license
C. Tap interface with the Decryption Port Mirror license
D. Decryption Mirror interface with the associated Decryption Port Mirror license

QUESTION 43

When is the content inspection done in the packet flow process?
A. after the application has been identified
B. before session lookup
C. before the packet forwarding process
D. after the SSL Proxy re-encrypts the packet

QUESTION 44

A supervisor has made an SSL Decryption policy rule that decrypts SSL sessions on any port. Which log entry can the supervisor use to verify that sessions are being decrypted?

A. In the details of the Traffic log entries
B. Decryption log
C. Data Filtering log
D. In the details of the Threat log entries

QUESTION 45

A supervisor has been requested to organize a Palo Alto Networks NGFW to give protection contrary to external hosts attempting to exploit a flaw in an operating system on an internal system.

Which Security Profile kind will prevent this attack?

A. Vulnerability Protection
B. Anti-Spyware
C. URL Filtering
D. Antivirus

QUESTION 46

What will be the egress interface if the traffic's ingress interface is ethernet1/6 sourcing from 192.168.111.3 and to the destination 10.46.41.113 for the duration of the time shown in the image?

```
admin@Lab33-111-PA-3060(active)> show clock

Thu Jun  8 12:49:55 PDT 2017
#####################
admin@Lab33-111-PA-3060(active)# show vsys vsys1 rulebase pbf rules test-pbf
test-pbf {
  action {
    forward {
      egress-interface ethernet1/5;
    }
  }
  from {
    zone L3-Trust;
  }
  enforce-symmetric-return {
    enabled no;
  }
  source 192.168.111.3;
  destination 10.46.41.113;
  source-user any;
  application any;
  service any;
  schedule schedule-pbf;
}
#####################
admin@Lab33-111-PA-3060(active)# show vsys vsys1 schedule schedule-pbf
schedule-pbf {
  schedule-type {
    recurring {
      daily 16:00-21:00;
    }
  }
}
#####################
admin@Lab33-111-PA-3060(active)> show routing fib
id   destination       nexthop       flags  interface    mtu
47   0.0.0.0/0         10.46.40.1    ug     ethernet1/3  1500
67   10.10.20.0/24     0.0.0.0       u      ethernet1/7  1500
66   10.10.20.111/32   0.0.0.0       uh     ethernet1/7  1500
46   10.46.40.0/23     0.0.0.0       u      ethernet1/3  1500
49   10.46.44.0/23     0.0.0.0       u      ethernet1/5  1500
45   10.46.41.111/32   0.0.0.0       uh     ethernet1/3  1500
70   10.46.41.113/32   10.46.40.1    ug     ethernet1/3  1500
48   10.46.45.111/32   0.0.0.0       uh     ethernet1/5  1500
51   192.168.111.0/24  0.0.0.0       u      ethernet1/6  1500
50   192.168.111.2/32  0.0.0.0       uh     ethernet1/6  1500
```

A. ethernet1/7
B. ethernet1/5
C. ethernet1/6
D. ethernet1/3

QUESTION 47

Signify to the display. A web server in the DMZ is being mapped to a public address through DNAT.

Which Security policy rule will let traffic to flow to the web server?

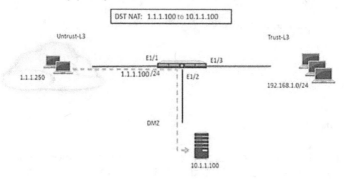

A. Untrust (any) to Untrust (10.1.1.100), web browsing – Let
B. Untrust (any) to Untrust (1.1.1.100), web browsing – Let
C. Untrust (any) to DMZ (1.1.1.100), web browsing – Let
D. Untrust (any) to DMZ (10.1.1.100), web browsing – Let

QUESTION 48

A web server is hosted in the DMZ and the server is arranged to listen for incoming connections on TCP port 443. A Security policies rules letting access from the Trust zone to the DMZ zone needs to be arranged to let web-browsing access. The web server hosts its contents over HTTP(S). Traffic from Trust to DMZ is being decrypted with a Forward Proxy rule.

Which combination of service and application, and order of Security policy rules, needs to be arranged to let cleartext web-browsing traffic to this server on tcp/443?

A. Rule #1: application: web-browsing; service: application-default; action: let Rule #2: application: ssl; service: application-default; action: let

B. Rule #1: application: web-browsing; service: service-http; action: let Rule #2: application: ssl; service: application-default; action: let

C. Rule # 1: application: ssl; service: application-default; action: let Rule #2: application: web-browsing; service: application-default; action: let

D. Rule #1: application: web-browsing; service: service-https; action: let Rule #2: application: ssl; service: application-default; action: let

QUESTION 49

A global corporate office has a large-scale network with only one User-ID agent, which makes a bottleneck near the User-ID agent server. Which solution in PAN-OS® software would help in this case?

A. application override

B. Virtual Wire mode

C. content inspection

D. redistribution of user mappings

QUESTION 50

Which two benefits come from assigning a Decryption Profile to a
Decryption policy rule with a "No Decrypt" action? (Select two.)

A. Block sessions with expired licenses
B. Block sessions with client verification
C. Block sessions with unsupported cipher suites
D. Block sessions with untrusted issuers
E. Block credential phishing

QUESTION 51

Which User-ID procedure must be arranged to map IP addresses to
usernames for users connected through a terminal server?

A. port mapping
B. server monitoring
C. client probing
D. XFF headers

QUESTION 52

Which attribute can be arranged on VM-Series firewalls?

A. aggregate interfaces
B. machine learning
C. numerous virtual systems
D. GlobalProtect

QUESTION 53

In High Availability, which information is transferred via the HA data link?

A. session information
B. heartbeats
C. HA state information
D. User-ID information

QUESTION 54

If a supervisor wants to decrypt SMTP traffic and possesses the server's license, which SSL decryption mode will let the Palo Alto Networks NGFW to inspect traffic to the server?

A. TLS Bidirectional Inspection
B. SSL Inbound Inspection
C. SSH Forward Proxy
D. SMTP Inbound Decryption

QUESTION 55

Which two procedures can be used to verify firewall connectivity to AutoFocus? (Select two.)

A. Verify AutoFocus status using the CLI "test" command.
B. Check the WebUI Dashboard AutoFocus widget.
C. Check for WildFire forwarding logs.
D. Check the license.
E. Verify AutoFocus is allowed below Device Management tab.

QUESTION 56

Which two subscriptions are available when configuring Panorama to push dynamic updates to connected devices? (Select two.)

A. Content-ID
B. User-ID
C. Applications and Threats
D. Antivirus

QUESTION 57

What is exchanged through the HA2 link?

A. hello heartbeats
B. User-ID information
C. session synchronization
D. HA state information

QUESTION 58

Which prerequisite needs to be satisfied before creating an SSH proxy Decryption policy?

A. Both SSH keys and SSL licenses needs to be generated.
B. No prerequisites are needed.
C. SSH keys needs to be manually generated.
D. SSL licenses needs to be generated.

QUESTION 59

VPN traffic intended for a supervisor's Palo Alto Networks NGFW is being maliciously intercepted and retransmitted by the interceptor. When creating a VPN tunnel, which protection profile can be allowed to prevent this malicious behavior?

A. Zone Protection
B. Replay
C. Web Application
D. DoS Protection

QUESTION 60

A supervisor has arranged a QoS policy rule and a QoS Profile that limits the maximum lettable bandwidth for the YouTube application. However, YouTube is consuming more than the maximum bandwidth allotment arranged.

Which arrangement step needs to be arranged to activate QoS?

A. Activate QoS interface
B. Activate QoS in the Interface Management Profile
C. Activate QoS Data Filtering Profile
D. Activate QoS monitor

QUESTION 61

Which log file can be used to classify SSL decryption failures?

A. Traffic
B. ACC
C. Arrangement
D. Threats

QUESTION 62

A customer wants to set up a site-to-site VPN using tunnel interfaces. Which two formats are accurate for naming tunnel interfaces? (Select two.)

A. tunnel.1
B. vpn-tunnel.1
C. tunnel.1025
D. vpn-tunnel.1024

QUESTION 63

A supervisor wants a new Palo Alto Networks NGFW to obtain automatic application updates daily, so it is arranged to use a scheduler for the application database. Unfortunately, they needed the management network to be isolated so that it cannot reach the Internet.

Which arrangement will activate the firewall to download and install application updates automatically?

A. Download and install application updates cannot be done automatically if the MGT port cannot reach the Internet.
B. Organize a service route for Palo Alto Networks Services that uses a dataplane interface that can route traffic to the Internet, and make a Security policy rule to let the traffic from that interface to the update servers if necessary.
C. Organize a Policy Based Forwarding policy rule for the update server IP address so that traffic sourced from the management interfaced destined for the update servers goes out of the interface acting as your Internet connection.
D. Organize a Security policy rule to let all traffic to and from the update servers.

QUESTION 64

A company wants to install a NGFW firewall among two core switches on a VLAN trunk link. They need to assign each VLAN to its own zone and to assign untagged (native) traffic to its own zone.

Which selection differentiates numerous VLANs into separate zones?

A. Make V-Wire objects with two V-Wire interfaces and define a range of "0-4096" in the "Tag Permitted" field of the V-Wire object.
B. Make V-Wire objects with two V-Wire subinterfaces and assign only a single VLAN ID to the "Tag Permitted" field of the V-Wire object. Repeat for every added VLAN and use a VLAN ID of 0 for untagged traffic. Assign each interface/subinterface to a unique zone.
C. Make Layer 3 subinterfaces that are each allotted to a single VLAN ID and a common virtual router. The physical Layer 3 interface would handle untagged traffic. Assign each interface/subinterface to a unique zone. Do not assign any interface an IP address.
D. Make VLAN objects for each VLAN and assign VLAN interfaces matching each VLAN ID. Repeat for every added VLAN and use a VLAN ID of 0 for untagged traffic. Assign each interface/subinterface to a unique zone.

QUESTION 65

Where can a supervisor see both the management plane and data plane CPU utilization in the WebUI?

A. System Utilization log
B. System log
C. Resources widget
D. CPU Utilization widget

QUESTION 66

Which four NGFW multi-factor verification factors are supported by PAN-OS®? (Select four.)

A. Short message service
B. Push
C. User logon
D. Voice
E. SSH key
F. One-Time Password

QUESTION 67

Which two attributes does PAN-OS® software use to classify applications? (Select two.)

A. transaction characteristics
B. session number
C. port number
D. application layer payload

QUESTION 68

A supervisor wants to upgrade an NGFW from PAN-OS® 7.1.2 to PAN-OS® 8.1.0. The firewall is not a part of an HA pair. What needs to be updated first?
A. Applications and Threats
B. XML Agent
C. WildFire
D. PAN-OS® Upgrade Agent

QUESTION 69

When backing up and saving arrangement files, what is achieved using only the firewall and is not available in Panorama?

A. Load arrangement version
B. Save candidate config
C. Export device state
D. Load named arrangement snapshot

QUESTION 70

A supervisor just submitted a newly found piece of spyware for WildFire analysis. The spyware passively monitors behavior without the user's knowledge. What is the expected verdict from WildFire?

A. Malware
B. Grayware
C. Phishing
D. Spyware

QUESTION 71

When configuring the firewall for packet capture, what are the authentic stage kinds?

A. receive, management, transmit, and non-syn
B. receive, management, transmit, and drop
C. receive, firewall, deliver, and non-syn
D. receive, firewall, transmit, and drop

QUESTION 72

Which User-ID procedure maps IP addresses to usernames for users connecting through a web proxy that has already authenticated the user?

A. syslog listening
B. server monitoring
C. client probing
D. port mapping

QUESTION 73

Which GlobalProtect Client connect procedure requires the distribution and use of machine licenses?

A. At-boot
B. Pre-logon
C. User-logon (Always on)
D. On-demand

QUESTION 74

Which attribute can give NGFWs with User-ID mapping information?

A. Web Captcha
B. Native 802.1q verification
C. GlobalProtect
D. Native 802.1x verification

QUESTION 75

Which Panorama supervisor kinds require the arrangement of at least one access domain? (Select two.)

A. Role Based
B. Custom Panorama Admin
C. Device Group
D. Dynamic
E. Template Admin

QUESTION 76

Which selection allows a Palo Alto Networks NGFW supervisor to program Application and Threat updates even applying only new content-IDs to traffic?

A. Select download-and-install
B. Select download-only
C. Select download-and-install, with "Deactivate new apps in content update" selected
D. Select deactivate application updates and select "Install only Threat updates"

QUESTION 77

Which is the maximum number of samples that can be submitted to WildFire per day, based on a WildFire subscription?
A. 10,000
B. 15,000
C. 7,500
D. 5,000

QUESTION 78

A supervisor needs to upgrade an NGFW to the most current version of PAN-OS® software. The given is occurring:
- Firewall has internet connectivity through e 1/1.
- Default security rules and security rules letting all SSL and web-
- browsing traffic to and from any zone. Service route is arranged, sourcing update traffic from e1/1.
- A communication error appears in the System logs when updates
- are done. Download does not complete.

What needs to be arranged to activate the firewall to download the current version of PAN-OS software?
A. Static route pointing application PaloAlto-updates to the update servers
B. Security policy rule letting PaloAlto-updates as the application
C. Scheduler for timed downloads of PAN-OS software
D. DNS settings for the firewall to use for resolution

QUESTION 79

A client has a sensitive application server in their data center and is specificly concerned about session flooding for the reason that of denial-of-service attacks. How can the Palo Alto Networks NGFW be arranged to specifically protect this server contrary to session floods originating from a single IP address?
A. Add an Anti-Spyware Profile to block attacking IP address
B. Define a custom App-ID to ensure that only legitimate application traffic reaches the server
C. Add QoS Profiles to throttle incoming requests
D. Add a tuned DoS Protection Profile

QUESTION 80

A supervisor deploys PA-500 NGFWs as an active/passive high availability pair. The devices are not participating in dynamic routing, and preemption is inactivated.

What needs to be verified to upgrade the firewalls to the most recent version of PAN-OS® software?

A. Antivirus update package.
B. Applications and Threats update package.
C. User-ID agent.
D. WildFire update package.

QUESTION 81

A firewall supervisor has been requested to organize a Palo Alto Networks NGFW to prevent contrary to compromised hosts trying to phone-home or beacon out to external command-and-control (C2) servers.

Which Security Profile kind will prevent these behaviors?

A. Anti-Spyware
B. WildFire
C. Vulnerability Protection
D. Antivirus

QUESTION 82

What must a supervisor consider when planning to revert Panorama to a pre-PAN-OS 8.1 version?

A. Panorama cannot be reverted to an earlier PAN-OS release if variables are used in templates or template piles.
B. A supervisor needs to use the Expedition tool to adapt the arrangement to the pre-PAN-OS 8.1 state.
C. When Panorama is reverted to an earlier PAN-OS release, variables used in templates or template piles will be removed automatically.
D. Supervisors need to manually update variable characters to those used in pre-PAN-OS 8.1.

QUESTION 83

Which administrative verification procedure supports authorization by an external service?

A. Licenses
B. LDAP
C. RADIUS
D. SSH keys

QUESTION 84

Which three file kinds can be forwarded to WildFire for analysis as a part of the basic WildFire service? (Select three.)

A. .dll
B. .exe
C. .fon
D. .apk
E. .pdf
F. .jar

QUESTION 85

A supervisor has been requested to organize active/active HA for a pair of Palo Alto Networks NGFWs. The firewall use Layer 3 interfaces to deliver traffic to a single gateway IP for the pair.

Which arrangement will activate this HA scenario?

A. The two firewalls will share a single floating IP and will use gratuitous ARP to share the floating IP.
B. Each firewall will have a separate floating IP, and importance will determine which firewall has the primary IP.
C. The firewalls do not use floating IPs in active/active HA.
D. The firewalls will share the same interface IP address, and device 1 will use the floating IP if device 0 fails.

QUESTION 86

How does Panorama prompt VMWare NSX to quarantine an infected VM?

A. HTTP Server Profile
B. Syslog Server Profile
C. Email Server Profile
D. SNMP Server Profile

QUESTION 87

Which two actions would be part of an automatic solution that would block sites with untrusted licenses without enabling SSL Forward Proxy? (Select two.)

A. Make a no-decrypt Decryption Policy rule.
B. Organize an EDL to pull IP addresses of known sites resolved from a CRL.
C. Organize a Dynamic Address Group for untrusted sites.
D. Make a Security Policy rule with a vulnerability Security Profile attached.
E. Activate the "Block sessions with untrusted issuers" setting.

QUESTION 88

SAML SLO is supported for which two firewall attributes? (Select two.)

A. GlobalProtect Portal
B. Captive Portal
C. WebUI
D. CLI

QUESTION 89

What are the two behavior differences among Highlight Unused Rules and the Rule Usage Hit counter when a firewall is rebooted? (Select two.)

A. Rule Usage Hit counter will not be reset
B. Highlight Unused Rules will highlight all rules.
C. Highlight Unused Rules will highlight zero rules.
D. Rule Usage Hit counter will reset.

QUESTION 90

Which is not an authentic reason for receiving a decrypt-cert-authentication error?

A. Unsupported HSM
B. Unknown license status
C. Client verification
D. Untrusted issuer

QUESTION 91

The firewall is not downloading IP addresses from MineMeld. Based on the image, what most likely is wrong?

A. A License Profile that comprises the client license needs to be selected.
B. The source address supports only files hosted with an ftp://<address/file>.
C. External Dynamic Lists do not support SSL connections.
D. A License Profile that comprises the CA license needs to be selected.

QUESTION 92

Which three split tunnel procedures are supported by a GlobalProtect Gateway? (Select three.)

A. video streaming application
B. Client Application Process
C. Destination Domain
D. Source Domain
E. Destination user/group
F. URL Category

QUESTION 93

Which selection describes the operation of the automatic commit recovery attribute?

A. It allows a firewall to revert to the previous arrangement if rule shadowing is detected.
B. It allows a firewall to revert to the previous arrangement if application dependency errors are found.
C. It allows a firewall to revert to the previous arrangement if a commit reasons HA partner connectivity failure.
D. It allows a firewall to revert to the previous arrangement if a commit reasons Panorama connectivity failure.

QUESTION 94

Which three items are important considerations for the duration of SD-WAN arrangement planning? (Select three.)

A. branch and hub locations
B. link necessities
C. the name of the ISP
D. IP Addresses

QUESTION 95

Starting with PAN-OS version 9.1, application dependency information is now reported in which two new locations? (Select two.)

A. on the **App Dependency** tab in the **Commit Status** window
B. on the Policy Optimizer's **Rule Usage** page
C. on the **Application** tab in the **Security Policy Rule** creation window
D. on the **Objects > Applications** browser pages

QUESTION 96

Panorama gives which two SD-WAN functions? (Select two.)

A. network monitoring
B. control plane
C. data plane
D. physical network links

ANSWERS

1. Correct Answer: C
2. Correct Answer: D

Reference:
https://www.paloaltonetworks.com/documentation/80/pan-os/pan-os/policy/security-profiles

3. Correct Answer: D

Reference: https://docs.paloaltonetworks.com/pan-os/7-1/pan-os-admin/high-availability/device-priority-and-preemption

4. Correct Answer: A
5. Correct Answer: D

Reference:
https://www.paloaltonetworks.com/documentation/80/pan-os/pan-os/policy/register-ip-addresses-and-tags-dynamically

6. Correct Answer: C
7. Correct Answer: BD

Reference: https://www.paloaltonetworks.com/products/secure-the-network/virtualized-next-generation-firewall/vm-series

8. Correct Answer: C
9. Correct Answer: B
10. Correct Answer: D
11. Correct Answer: B

Reference:
https://www.paloaltonetworks.com/documentation/80/pan-os/pan-os/authentication/configure-multi-factor-authentication

12. Correct Answer: A
13. Correct Answer: C

Reference: https://live.paloaltonetworks.com/t5/Configuration-Articles/How-to-Change-the-Speed-and-Duplex-of-the-Management-Port/ta-p/59034

14. Correct Answer: A
15. Correct Answer: D
16. Correct Answer: C
17. Correct Answer: D

Reference: https://live.paloaltonetworks.com/t5/Learning-Articles/How-to-Run-a-Packet-Capture/ta-p/62390

18. Correct Answer: D
Reference:
https://www.paloaltonetworks.com/documentation/80/pan-os/pan-os/quality-of-service/qos-concepts/qos-for-applications-and-users#idaed4e749-80b4- 4641-a37c-c741aba562e9

19. Correct Answer: B
20. Correct Answer: B
21. Correct Answer: BC
22. Correct Answer: ABC
23. Correct Answer: B
24. Correct Answer: A
25. Correct Answer: A
Reference: https://docs.paloaltonetworks.com/pan-os/9-1/pan-os-new-features/globalprotect-features/enhanced-logging-for-globalprotect.html

26. Correct Answer: ACF
27. Correct Answer: A
Reference: https://live.paloaltonetworks.com/t5/Configuration-Articles/Failed-to-Block-Facebook-Chat-Consistently/ta-p/115673

28. Correct Answer: A
29. Correct Answer: B
30. Correct Answer: B
31. Correct Answer: A
32. Correct Answer: D
Reference:
https://www.paloaltonetworks.com/documentation/80/pan-os/web-interface-help/device/device-certificate-management-ssltls-service-profile

33. Correct Answer: C
Reference: https://live.paloaltonetworks.com/t5/Management-Articles/How-To-Packet-Capture-tcpdump-On-Management-Interface/ta-p/55415

34. Correct Answer: B
Reference: https://live.paloaltonetworks.com/t5/Management-Articles/Tips-amp-Tricks-How-to-Use-the-Application-Command-Center-ACC/ta-p/67342

35. Correct Answer: CDE

36. Correct Answer: A
Reference:
https://www.paloaltonetworks.com/documentation/80/pan-os/pan-os/threat-prevention/prevent-credential-phishing

37. Correct Answer: D
Reference:
https://www.paloaltonetworks.com/documentation/71/panorama/panorama_adminguide/administer-panorama/back-up-panorama-and-firewall- configurations

38. Correct Answer: CD

39. Correct Answer: AB

40. Correct Answer: ADE
Reference:
https://www.paloaltonetworks.com/documentation/71/pan-os/pan-os/high-availability/ha-firewall-states

41. Correct Answer: C
Reference:
https://www.paloaltonetworks.com/documentation/80/pan-os/pan-os/policy/policy-based-forwarding/pbf/path-monitoring-for-pbf

42. Correct Answer: D
Reference:
https://www.paloaltonetworks.com/documentation/80/pan-os/pan-os/decryption/decryption-concepts/decryption-mirroring

43. Correct Answer: A
Reference:
https://live.paloaltonetworks.com/t5/Learning-Articles/Packet-Flow-Sequence-in-PAN-OS/ta-p/56081

44. Correct Answer: A
Reference: https://live.paloaltonetworks.com/t5/Configuration-Articles/How-to-Implement-and-Test-SSL-Decryption/ta-p/59719

45. Correct Answer: A
Reference:
https://www.paloaltonetworks.com/documentation/80/pan-os/web-interface-help/objects/objects-security-profiles-vulnerability-protection

46. Correct Answer: D
47. Correct Answer: C
48. Correct Answer: A
49. Correct Answer: D
Reference:
https://www.paloaltonetworks.com/documentation/80/pan-os/pan-os/user-id/deploy-user-id-in-a-large-scale-network

50. Correct Answer: AD
Reference:
https://www.paloaltonetworks.com/documentation/80/pan-os/pan-os/decryption/define-traffic-to-decrypt/create-a-decryption-profile

51. Correct Answer: A
Reference:
https://www.paloaltonetworks.com/documentation/71/pan-os/pan-os/user-id/configure-user-mapping-for-terminal-server-users

52. Correct Answer: D
53. Correct Answer: A
Reference:
https://www.paloaltonetworks.com/documentation/80/pan-os/pan-os/high-availability/ha-concepts/ha-links-and-backup-links

54. Correct Answer: B
Reference:
https://www.paloaltonetworks.com/documentation/80/pan-os/pan-os/decryption/configure-ssl-inbound-inspection

55. Correct Answer: DE
Reference:
https://www.paloaltonetworks.com/documentation/80/pan-os/pan-os/getting-started/enable-autofocus-threat-intelligence

56. Correct Answer: CD
Reference:
https://www.paloaltonetworks.com/documentation/80/pan-os/web-interface-help/device/device-dynamic-updates

57. Correct Answer: C

Reference:
https://www.paloaltonetworks.com/documentation/80/pan-os/pan-os/high-availability/ha-concepts/ha-links-and-backup-links

58. Correct Answer: B
Reference:
https://www.paloaltonetworks.com/documentation/80/pan-os/pan-os/decryption/configure-ssh-proxy

59. Correct Answer: A
60. Correct Answer: A
61. Correct Answer: A
62. Correct Answer: AC
63. Correct Answer: B
64. Correct Answer: C
65. Correct Answer: C
66. Correct Answer: ABDF
Reference:
https://www.paloaltonetworks.com/documentation/80/pan-os/pan-os/authentication/configure-multi-factor-authentication

67. Correct Answer: AD
68. Correct Answer: C
69. Correct Answer: C
70. Correct Answer: B
71. Correct Answer: D
72. Correct Answer: A
73. Correct Answer: B
74. Correct Answer: C
75. Correct Answer: CE
76. Correct Answer: A
77. Correct Answer: A
78. Correct Answer: D
79. Correct Answer: D
80. Correct Answer: B
Reference:
https://www.paloaltonetworks.com/documentation/80/pan-os/newfeaturesguide/upgrade-to-pan-os-80/upgrade-the-firewall-to-pan-os-80/upgrade-an-ha- firewall-pair-to-pan-os-80

81. Correct Answer: A
Reference:
https://www.paloaltonetworks.com/documentation/71/pan-

os/pan-os/policy/anti-spyware-profiles

82. Correct Answer: A
Reference:
https://www.paloaltonetworks.com/documentation/81/pan-os/newfeaturesguide/upgrade-to-pan-os-81/upgradedowngrade-considerations

83. Correct Answer: C
Reference:
https://www.paloaltonetworks.com/documentation/80/pan-os/pan-os/firewall-administration/manage-firewall-administrators/administrative-authentication

84. Correct Answer: DEF
85. Correct Answer: A
Reference:
https://www.paloaltonetworks.com/documentation/71/pan-os/pan-os/high-availability/floating-ip-address-and-virtual-mac-address

86. Correct Answer: A
Reference:
https://www.paloaltonetworks.com/documentation/80/virtualization/virtualization/set-up-the-vm-series-firewall-on-vmware-nsx/dynamically-quarantine- infected-guests

87. Correct Answer: AD
Reference:
https://www.paloaltonetworks.com/documentation/71/pan-os/web-interface-help/objects/objects-decryption-profile

88. Correct Answer: AB
Reference:
https://www.paloaltonetworks.com/documentation/80/pan-os/pan-os/authentication/configure-saml-authentication

89. Correct Answer: AB
90. Correct Answer: A
Reference:
https://www.paloaltonetworks.com/documentation/71/pan-os/newfeaturesguide/networking-features/ssl-ssh-session-end-reasons

91. Correct Answer: D

Reference: https://live.paloaltonetworks.com/t5/MineMeld-
Articles/Connecting-PAN-OS-to-MineMeld-using-External-
Dynamic-Lists/ta-p/190414

92. Correct Answer: ABC

Reference:
https://www.paloaltonetworks.com/documentation/81/pan-
os/newfeaturesguide/globalprotect-features/split-tunnel-for-
public-applications

93. Correct Answer: D

Reference: https://docs.paloaltonetworks.com/pan-os/9-1/pan-os-
new-features/panorama-features/automatic-panorama-
connection-recovery.html

94. Correct Answer: ABD

Reference: https://docs.paloaltonetworks.com/sd-wan/1-0/sd-wan-
admin/sd-wan-overview/plan-sd-wan-configuration

95. Correct Answer: AC

Reference: https://docs.paloaltonetworks.com/pan-os/9-1/pan-os-
admin/app-id/use-application-objects-in-policy/resolve-
application-dependencies

96. Correct Answer: BC